Face Ache

Nicholas de Hirsching and Roser Capdevila

A&C Black · London

Published 1991 by A & C Black (Publishers) Limited
35 Bedford Row, London, WC1R 4JH

First published in 1989 in France by Editions Rouge et Or
under the title 'la grimassouille'.

Translated by Anne Watts.

A CIP catalogue record for this book
is available from the British Library.

ISBN 0–7136–3372–7

Text © 1989 Nicholas de Hirsching
Illustrations © 1989 Roser Capdevila

This edition copyright © 1991
A & C Black (Publishers) Limited

Filmset by August Filmsetting, Haydock, St Helens
Printed in Hong Kong by Wing King Tong Co. Ltd.

Watch out! Face Ache's about!
Avoid it like the plague!
Run for cover!

Little Vicky West started it all.
One morning she woke up with a
slight temperature and started to
behave very strangely. She rolled
her eyes as if she were drunk.
Then she stuck her finger right up
her nose . . .

. . . so far that it looked like she was trying to scratch her brains! Her parents were worried and called Doctor Robbins.

The doctor examined Vicky. 'Face Ache!' he groaned. 'Mrs West all your family *must* stay indoors.'

'Why? What for? What's wrong?' exclaimed Mr and Mrs West.

The doctor explained. 'It's VEC – Very Easy to Catch. Luckily it doesn't last long, but people who catch it can't stop making faces.'

He pointed at Vicky – who was trying to lick her nose.

'You see what I mean,' he said.

It might have all stopped there.
Vicky was thrilled not to have to go
to school, and her parents took a
day off work too.

But at lunch time, Mrs West
discovered that she'd run out of
bread. She stared at herself in the
mirror and decided . . .

'Piffle! I don't look ill. I can nip
out for five minutes.'

She ran to the baker, but as soon as she got there . . . disaster! She couldn't control herself.

She stuck her tongue out, then flicked it in and out like a snake, while pulling her ears.

The baker was amazed. 'Mrs West!
What has got into you?' he
burst out. 'You should change
your job and become a clown!'

Mrs West turned bright red. She picked up her French bread, paid and rushed home. But it was too late . . .

Quarter of an hour later, the baker started to feel funny. When he served his customers, he showed his teeth like a vampire and leered horribly.

After a few minutes all his
customers had run away. The
baker didn't understand what
had come over him. He shut
the shop, took an aspirin and went
to bed to try to forget his
dreadful day.

But the Face Ache was
spreading . . .

Every one of the baker's
customers was carrying the
germ. And every single one
passed it on to their family,
friends and neighbours.

Soon the town, then the whole
country, was split between Face
Achers and normal people who
couldn't understand what was
going on – which meant
problems . . .

Thousands of people were
sacked from their jobs. A lot of
others were called mad. Others
had the bad luck to ask
directions from policemen,
with their tongues stuck out!
They were arrested and taken
to the police station.

Shy people thought the Face
Achers were mocking them – so
they thumped the Face Achers.
But then they caught the
disease and it was their turn to
get thumped.

Shopkeepers couldn't sell anything and had to shut their shops. Nobody could work normally. It was a disaster!

That evening it was so bad that on the television the presenter was making crazy faces.

He interviewed a famous and very clever doctor with a big hairy beard.

The doctor explained that Face Ache was very easy to catch, but the germ could not stand the heat.

Because the weather forecast for the following afternoon was bright sunshine, the nasty germ would disappear very quickly.

The doctor explained this calmly except for sticking his fingers in his ears and wiggling his jaw from side to side like a cow chewing the cud.

So now everyone knew what was going on and life could continue as if nothing had happened.

So, to be a good example, the Prime Minister went to open a new theatre.

He made a speech while puffing out his cheeks and blinking like a frog. But it didn't stop the speech being a great success.

In the street people made faces when they met. Some of them were embarrassed and stared at the ground. But others had fun playing around.

Drivers started making long
noses at policemen! Children
stuck their tongues out at their
teachers – but the teachers were
very happy to do it back!

Then, something amazing happened. For the first time anyone could remember, the weather forecast was right! The sun shone brilliantly.

And all the people with Face Ache began to get better.

Some of them went on making
faces because it was fun, but the
plague quickly slowed down,
then disappeared.

That evening, the news reader, whose face had stopped twitching, announced: 'The Face Ache has ended. The terrible germ has stopped infecting the country.'

The doctor with the beard said: 'Tomorrow everything will go back to normal. Not a single Face Ache microbe is still alive. This is a scientific fact!'

The whole country breathed a sigh of relief and went to sleep peacefully.

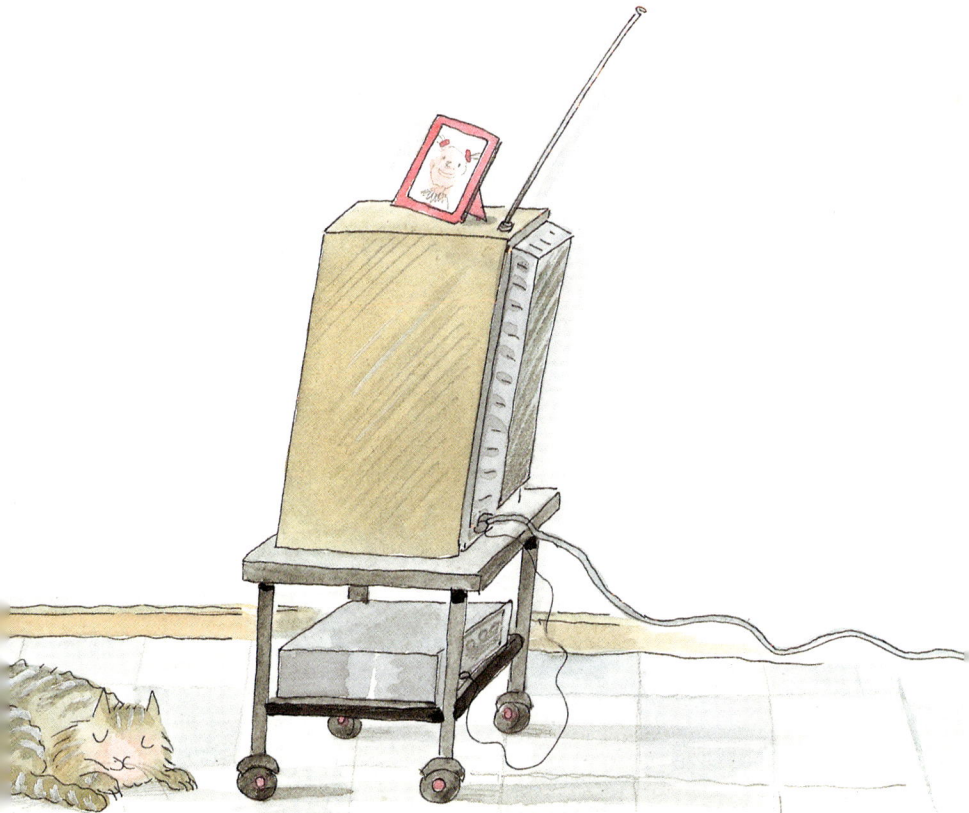

Which is the end of the Face
Ache story. Well, almost . . .

The next day, when Mrs West
woke Vicky up, she had a
terrible shock . . .

Vicky looked as though someone
had painted her all the colours
of the rainbow: green nose,
blue ears, orange cheeks,
purple chin.

She turned to her mother with a
big smile. 'Guess what, Mum,'
she sighed. 'Now I've caught
Colourpox!'